PU

Novice Guide To Ultimate & Proper Planting Techniques, Care & More

URIAH SEKANI

It is prohibited to reproduce, distribute, or transmit any portion of this publication, regardless of format or medium, without the publisher's written consent. However, the Copyright Law permits limited excerpts for evaluation and authorized noncommercial uses.

Copyright © 2023 By Uriah Sekani

All Rights Reserved

Table of Contents

INTRODUCTORY 5

CHAPTER ONE 10

  Importance Of Pumpkins Cultivation ...10

  A Survey Of Pumpkin Types 14

CHAPTER TWO 20

  The Pumpkin Life Cycle Explained 20

  How To Find The Best Pumpkin Patch Location 25

CHAPTER THREE 30

  Getting The Ground Ready For Pumpkin Seeds 30

  Careful Thoughts On Rare Pumpkins....35

CHAPTER FOUR 41

  Pumpkin Seed Germination 41

  Positioning Of Plants 47

CHAPTER FIVE 52

  How To Maintain Your Pumpkin Plants52

  The Gathering And Keeping Of Pumpkins 58

CHAPTER SIX 64

Making Use Of Pumpkins 64

Fixing The Most Frequent Pumpkin Issues 69

CHAPTER SEVEN 74

Modern Methods For Growing Pumpkins 74

Conclusion 81

THE END 84

INTRODUCTORY

Growing pumpkins, which are huge, spherical fruits in the Cucurbitaceae family, is known as pumpkin gardening. Pumpkins are cultivated for a wide range of functions, from food and decoration to animal fodder. They can be used in a variety of ways and are a common crop all around the world.

Here's a little primer on growing pumpkins:

• Choosing the Right Variety There are many different types of pumpkins, each with its own set of desirable qualities and practical applications. Pick one that fits your needs in terms of size, color, flavor, and time to maturity.

• Growing pumpkins successfully calls for a pH range of 6.0 to 7.5 in fertile, well-drained soil. Get rid of any weeds or trash that may be there to begin. Soil fertility and structure can be enhanced by adding organic matter like compost or well-rotted manure.

• Pumpkins are normally grown from seeds that are either placed directly into the ground or started inside and transplanted later. The best time to plant is conditional on where you live and the weather you can expect. The soil needs to be at least 60 degrees

Fahrenheit (15 degrees Celsius) before you can plant anything in it.

• Pumpkins are fast-growing plants that necessitate wide-ranging territory. Depending on the variety's height and spread, plant the seeds or transplants in hills or mounds spaced approximately 4 to 8 feet (1.2 to 2.4 meters) apart. There should be three to four seeds or plants in each hill.

• Fertilizing and watering the soil regularly will ensure a healthy plant growth. Water is crucial for pumpkins, especially during the fruit's development. If you want your plants to flourish, use an organic or balanced fertilizer and apply it as directed.

- Controlling Pests and illnesses Aphids, cucumber beetles, powdery mildew, and squash vine borers are just some of the pests and illnesses that pumpkins may be susceptible to. Keep an eye on your crops and take preventative steps like applying organic insecticides, row coverings, or crop rotation as needed.

- Pollination is necessary for pumpkins to produce fruit. Pollen must be transferred from male to female flowers, and this can only happen with the help of pollinators like bees. You can either put in some flowering plants in the area or use a little paintbrush to pollinate the flowers yourself.

• Pumpkins are ready to be harvested when their rinds are hard and the fruits have attained the desired size and color, but this varies by variety. If you want your fruit to last longer, leave the stems on. Remove the pumpkins from the vine by cutting them off using pruning shears or a knife.

For more particular advice on pumpkin production, make sure to check out gardening guides and speak with seasoned producers in your area.

CHAPTER ONE
Importance Of Pumpkins Cultivation

Growing pumpkins is a popular hobby for many people. Some popular reasons for producing pumpkins are as follows:

- Pumpkins have many culinary applications and are hence not just a Halloween staple for carving. Soups, pies, bread, and even savory foods might benefit from their inclusion. Freshly harvested pumpkins are preferred by many for their greater flavor and texture compared to those found in grocery stores.

- Decorating with pumpkins is a common fall tradition because pumpkins are such universal symbols of the season. You may use them to make lovely autumn displays, as festive table centerpieces, or even jack-o'-lanterns for Halloween. If you grow your own pumpkins for Halloween decorations, you may give them a special touch that no one else will have.

- Growing pumpkins is a rewarding experience that may teach both kids and adults new skills. It's a great way to pick up knowledge on gardening, plant biology, and other related topics.

Growing pumpkins from seed to table may be a fun and satisfying activity.

• Growing pumpkins is a great way to get involved in your community and meet new people. Many communities host pumpkin festivals when friends and family can get together to celebrate the harvest by picking their own pumpkins. Growing pumpkins may be a fun and bonding activity for the whole neighborhood.

• Pumpkins are a good source of nutrition for pigs and hens, among other livestock. When other forage alternatives are scarce in the fall, they can be used as a supplemental food source because of their high nutrient content.

• Seeing the results of one's hard work in the garden can be personally rewarding for many gardeners. Pumpkins, with their big, colorful fruits, can be a lot of fun to grow. Growing pumpkins effectively may be a satisfying and rewarding experience.

Growing pumpkins has several advantages, including culinary pleasure, decorative value, educational possibilities, and social interaction. Growing pumpkins can be a fun and profitable hobby whether you have a tiny balcony garden or a sprawling farm.

A Survey Of Pumpkin Types

There are many different types of pumpkins, each having its own unique size, color, form, flavor, and culinary applications. Here's a rundown of some of the most well-liked pumpkin types:

• Pumpkins carved in the shape of a Jack-o'-lantern are a Halloween staple. They are perfect for constructing frightening patterns because of their round form, dark orange color, and thick walls. "Howden," "Connecticut Field," and "Cinderella" are just a few examples.

- Pumpkins of the sugar, or pie, variety are highly sought after because their flesh is sweet and flavorful, making them perfect for use in desserts, soups, and other baked items.

They are less fibrous and have a smoother texture than regular pumpkins. The 'Small Sugar,' 'Baby Pam,' and 'New England Pie' pumpkins are all great examples of the sugar pumpkin category.

- Grown specifically for their massive size, giant pumpkins are frequently submitted into contests. They can get incredibly heavy, often weighing over a thousand pounds.

Growers of huge pumpkins sometimes choose from among the 'Atlantic huge' and 'Dill's Atlantic Giant' kinds.

• Pumpkins that are pure white, rather than the more common orange, are gaining in popularity. They can be found in a wide range of sizes and forms, all of which lend a sophisticated air to autumnal displays. A few are 'Casper,' 'Lumina,' and 'Baby Boo.'

• Pumpkins of the heirloom variety are treasured for their special qualities and long history. Most of the time, they have been passed down through the generations and are open-pollinated. The heirloom pumpkin cultivars 'Jarrahdale,' 'Blue Hubbard,' and 'Long Island Cheese' are all quite popular.

• Pumpkins specifically bred for their beauty are called ornamental pumpkins. They can be found in a rainbow of hues and a wide range of sizes and textures, from tiny to lumpy. Popular varieties of decorative pumpkins used in autumn decorations, centerpieces, and crafts include 'Knucklehead,' 'Baby Boo,' and 'Munchkin.

• Cushaw pumpkins are easily identifiable by their distinctive crooked neck and bulbous base. They can be found in a rainbow of hues, from green to orange to white. Pies, casseroles, and preserves are common uses for Cushaw pumpkins. The 'Green Striped Cushaw' and the 'Tennessee Sweet Potato' are two popular selections.

• Some types of pumpkins have been developed for their edible properties. These cultivars are perfect for roasting, mashing, and pureeing because to their smooth texture and delicious flavor. The 'Musquee de Provence,' 'Rouge Vif d'Etampes,' and 'Cinderella pumpkin,' are just a few examples.

These pumpkins are only a small sampling of the numerous available. Consider your needs, preferences in flavor, and growth conditions while deciding on a pumpkin type.

CHAPTER TWO
The Pumpkin Life Cycle Explained

Pumpkins have a life cycle similar to that of other plants, beginning with seed germination and ending with seed production. A pumpkin goes through the following phases during its development:

• When a pumpkin seed germinates, a new life cycle begins. The radicle, also known as the root, emerges from the seed when it grows in size after absorbing water. The radicle extends underground to act as a root and a source of nourishment for the plant.

- As the radicle grows, the plant enters the seedling stage. Until the real leaves emerge, the seedling relies on its one or two cotyledons (seed leaves) for nutrition and energy. The first genuine leaves, which emerge after the cotyledons, are often bigger and more distinctive in shape.

- The pumpkin plant's leaves and stems are its primary focus throughout the vegetative growth phase. Because photosynthesis is so important to the plant's development and growth, the plant responds by producing more leaves and increasing the size of its foliage. The roots keep expanding downward and outward in search of moisture and nourishment.

• When the pumpkin plant has reached full maturity, it will begin to bloom. Male and female pumpkin blossoms develop on different plants. Male flowers, also known as peduncles, are responsible for pollination. Pumpkins have the ability to develop from the female flowers, which can be recognised by a little fruit (ovary) at the base.

• Pumpkins require pollination to set the stage for fruit development. Fertilization requires pollen from male flowers to reach female flowers. Bees and other pollinators travel from blossom to flower spreading their genetic material. Once the ovary has been fertilized with pollen, pumpkin development begins.

• Changes in color, size, and texture occur in a pumpkin as it matures. As it ages, the skin or rind hardens and becomes more rigid. The time it takes for a pumpkin to mature varies greatly from one variety to the next and from one set of growth conditions to another. Fruits develop healthily when given regular watering, enough sunlight, and a balanced diet.

• Pumpkins are ready for harvest when they have attained the desired size, color, and maturity. The pumpkin should have a hard rind and a completely dried stem where it was attached to the vine. Carefully pick the pumpkins while still keeping a short stem attached. The pumpkins' storage life can be lengthened through careful handling and storage after harvest.

- Pumpkins, if left to ripen for an extended period of time, will begin to degrade, and the seeds within will develop and harden. Allow the pumpkin to ripen completely, and then remove the seeds to store for next year's planting. The seeds should be washed and dried completely before being stored in a cool, dry area until the following spring.

If you want to harvest a bumper crop of pumpkins, you need to have a firm grasp of the plant's growth cycle.

How To Find The Best Pumpkin Patch Location

The health and development of your pumpkin plants depend on your careful consideration of potential farming locations. Here are some things to think about when planting pumpkins:

- Sunlight: Pumpkins can't grow without a lot of exposure to natural light. Pick a spot that gets at least six to eight hours of direct sunlight daily. Don't hang around in shadowy spots created by nearby buildings, trees, or other obstacles.

- Pumpkins thrive in fertile, well-drained soil with a pH of 6.0 to 7.5. Find out what nutrients and pH level the soil has by doing a soil test. To boost its fertility, structure, and water-holding ability, soil can be amended with organic matter such as compost or well-rotted manure.

- Root rot and other plant diseases can be avoided by ensuring the selected site has adequate water drainage. To prevent flooding, stay away from places that have heavy clay soil.

- Protect the pumpkin vines from the wind, as it might cause harm and prevent pollination. Think about picking a spot that is shielded from the wind by existing structures, barriers, or tall trees.

- Pumpkins are fast-developing vine crops that need lots of room to spread out. Select a location that is large enough to house all of the plants you intend to grow, with room to spare. This will keep things from getting too crowded, increase ventilation, and make it simpler to perform necessary tasks like upkeep and harvesting.

- Water Availability: A steady supply of water is essential for pumpkin production. It's important to pick a location close to a water source or irrigation system that can deliver enough water for the entire growing season, even dry spells.

• If at all possible, select a location with a limited record of pest and disease infestations. If pests or illnesses have been a problem in recent crops or in the neighboring vegetation, you should look elsewhere to plant your pumpkins.

• Pumpkin-specific pests and diseases can be reduced by rotating crops every few years. To reduce the likelihood of recurrence, choose a location where pumpkins have not been planted for at least three to four years, or rotate with unrelated crops.

• Think about how far you'd have to go to get to your house or storage facility from the property. Being able to easily check on the pumpkin patch makes it much simpler to care for the plants, especially during the flowering and fruiting phases.

If you give these considerations, you'll be able to pick a location for your pumpkin farm that will guarantee healthy plants and a plentiful harvest.

CHAPTER THREE
Getting The Ground Ready For Pumpkin Seeds

It's crucial to have the soil in good condition before planting pumpkins so that the plants can thrive. Here are the measures to take before planting pumpkins:

• Get Rid of Weeds, Rocks, and Debris First, clear the area where you wish to plant. This will aid in making sure the pumpkin plants don't have to fight over resources like water and food.

• Dig the soil up to a depth of 8 to 12 inches (20 to 30 cm) with a garden fork or tiller. This will enhance the soil's ability to breathe, drain, and accept root growth. Over-tilling can cause soil compaction, thus it's best to avoid doing it.

• Amend the soil with compost, aged manure, or other organic materials if it is deficient in organic matter or nutrients. Add some organic material, like as compost, to the top few inches (or centimeters) of soil and work it in. The soil's fertility, ability to hold water, and structure will all improve as a result.

• Determine the soil's pH through testing, then make any necessary adjustments. Soil with a pH between 6.0 and 7.5 is ideal for pumpkin cultivation. If the results of the soil test show that the pH is too high or low, you may need to make adjustments by adding lime or sulfur.

• Fertilizer should be worked into the soil before planting using the method indicated by the fertilizer's manufacturer. The developing pumpkins will benefit greatly from this. For optimal plant growth, select a fertilizer with a N:P:K ratio of 10:10:10 or 14:14:14.

• Use a garden rake to even out the soil and create a flat surface. This will make it easier to irrigate the land and produce a level planting bed.

- Build Mounds or Hills Raise the soil by building mounds or hills around your pumpkin plants to increase drainage and hasten the warming of the soil. Gather soil to make mounds or hills, 1 to 2 feet (30 to 60 cm) in diameter and 6 to 8 inches (15 to 20 cm) high. Spread the hills or mounds apart as instructed by the seed packet for the pumpkins you intend to grow.

•. Wait for the Soil to Settle: After you've worked the soil, wait a few days before planting. This will allow the soil to stabilize after any disruptions were made during the preparation procedure.

Having the soil properly prepared can allow pumpkin plants to flourish by encouraging strong root growth. Soil preparation measures should be modified to account for local conditions and the type of pumpkin you wish to plant.

Careful Thoughts On Rare Pumpkins

Growing unique pumpkin types requires attention to a few extra details. When opposed to common pumpkins, specialty varieties sometimes have specific preferences or needs. Growing unique pumpkin types requires attention to the following details:

• Identify the specialized pumpkin kinds you're interested in growing, then choose among them. It's possible that the growing habits, fruit size, color, and flavor of each variety are unique. Market demand, your intended audience, and your own preferences are all important considerations when selecting specialized cultivars.

• Demand in the Market Do some research into how popular your intended specialized pumpkin types are likely to be. Miniature pumpkins and white pumpkins, for example, may be in higher demand due to their ornamental and/or culinary potential. A prosperous harvest can be ensured by keeping up with market tendencies and consumer preferences.

• Think about the pumpkin kinds you want to plant, and how much room you can give each one to spread out. There are kinds with compact vines and others with aggressive growth that need more room to spread. If you want your plants to thrive and bear fruit, you need to provide them room to do so.

• Different varieties of speciality pumpkins may have different soil and fertilization needs. Soil drainage is important for some plants, but others may grow in heavy or sandy environments. Test the soil's fertility and pH to see what adjustments need to be made to meet the needs of your speciality plant kinds of choice.

• Some specialized types of pumpkin can only be grown in a certain range of temperatures, or during a certain time of year. Think about the typical weather patterns and duration of the growth season in your area. Be sure that the time of year and temperature range ideal for your selected speciality crops.

• Disease and Pest Control: There may be a range of resistance in specialty pumpkin types. Develop a thorough strategy for controlling pests and illnesses by learning what kinds of problems are typical for the particular types you're producing. This may involve organic or chemical controls, as well as regular scouting and preventative measures, cultural traditions, and so on.

- Harvesting and Care: Pumpkins produced for specific reasons, such as decoration or cooking, are known as "specialty pumpkins." It's important to know when to harvest your crop, as this varies by type and end use. Carefully handling the speciality pumpkins will keep their quality and look intact.

- If you intend to cultivate unique pumpkin types for commercial purposes, you should give some thought to how you intend to advertise and sell your harvest. Research local markets, restaurants, and specialty stores to see if they might be interested in purchasing the specialty pumpkins you are cultivating. If you put in the time and effort now, you should have a much easier time selling your speciality pumpkins when the time comes.

Taking these into account and adapting your strategy to the needs of the speciality pumpkin types you select will help you achieve your goals and satisfy your target market.

CHAPTER FOUR
Pumpkin Seed Germination

Planting pumpkin seeds indoors and then transferring the seedlings to the garden gives the plants a head start and increases the likelihood of a fruitful harvest. Here is a detailed tutorial on how to germinate pumpkin seeds:

- The best time to plant pumpkin seeds is two to four weeks before the latest frost date in your location. The seedlings can have a good head start on their growth before being moved to the garden.

- Select Containers: Use containers with drainage holes, such as seed starting trays, plastic pots, or biodegradable peat pots. Make sure the containers are free of debris and have enough room for the roots to expand.

• To start seeds, fill containers with a seed starting mix that has adequate drainage and can hold some moisture. Put the mixture into the containers, stopping about half an inch (1.3 cm) from the top.

• Plant Two or Three Pumpkin Seeds in Each Pot. Dig a hole about 1 inch (2.5 cm) deep by pressing down with your finger or a pencil. The seeds should be dropped into the hole and the earth should be carefully packed around them.

• The optimal germination temperature for pumpkin seeds is between 75 and 85 degrees Fahrenheit (24 and 29 degrees Celsius). Store the containers someplace warm, like on top of the fridge or next to a heating pad. Mist the soil or use a spray bottle to keep it moist so it doesn't dry out.

• Once the seedlings sprout, they will need a lot of light in order to thrive. If natural light is insufficient, supplement it with fluorescent grow lights by placing the plants in an area where they will receive at least 6 to 8 hours of sunlight every day.

- When the seedlings have two or three genuine leaves, thin them by removing the weaker seedlings so that you are left with only one plant per container before transplanting. The remaining seedling will now have plenty of room to expand. When thinning, take care not to damage the roots.

- Acclimate the seedlings to outside circumstances for about a week before putting them in the garden. Start by exposing them to sunlight and wind for short periods of time each day for a week in a covered outside area.

- Once the threat of frost has gone and the seedlings have hardened off, they can be planted in the garden. The pumpkin plants require a sunny spot with loose, well-drained soil and plenty of room to grow.

• Dig holes in the garden bed only slightly bigger than the root ball of each seedling and place them at the appropriate distance apart. Plant your pumpkins with the recommended distances between them for that particular kind. Plants should have about 3–5 feet (1–1.5 meters) of space between them, and rows should have about 6–8 feet (1.8–2.4 meters) of space between them.

• After planting, give the seedlings plenty of water and cover the ground around them with a layer of organic mulch. Mulching serves to control soil temperature, prevent weed development, and preserve moisture.

Getting your pumpkin plants off to a strong start in the house before transferring them to the garden is as easy as following these instructions.

Positioning Of Plants

The success of your pumpkin crop depends on how far apart you put your seedlings in the garden. How to plant pumpkin seeds and determine their spacing:

1. Select a spot in your garden that gets at least six to eight hours of sunlight a day for optimal growth. Pumpkins need a lot of sunlight to grow and produce healthy fruit.

2. First, loosen the soil to a depth of 8 to 12 inches (20 to 30 cm) before planting. To enhance soil fertility and structure, get rid of weeds and debris and add in some organic material like compost or well-rotted manure.

3. The ideal planting depth is between 1 and 2 inches (2.5 and 5 cm). Spread out two or three pumpkin seeds in each hole. Put some soil over the seeds and pat it down carefully.

4. Guidelines for place SpacingPumpkin varieties and vine growth habits determine how far apart to place individual plants. Some broad rules of thumb are as follows:

• Plants of vining types ought to be set at a distance of 6-10 feet (1.8-3 meters) apart in rows, with the rows themselves being set at a distance of 8-12 feet (2.4-3.6 meters) apart. This promotes vine growth and reduces congestion.

• Plant semi-bush and bush kinds 3–5 feet (1–1.5 meters) apart, and leave

1.8–2.4 meters between rows. Even though these types take up less room, they still need some breathing room.

• Space plants 3 to 4 feet (0.9 to 1.2 meters) apart in rows that are 3 to 4 feet (0.6 to 0.9 meters) apart. o For miniature or ornamental kinds, space plants 2 to 3 feet (0.6 to 0.9 meters) apart. Due to their compact growth, these smaller types can be planted more densely.

5. If more than one seed sprouts in a given planting hole, thin the seedlings when they have two or three genuine leaves. Take out the less robust seedlings and replace them with only the strongest ones. By removing unnecessary plants, you give the surviving ones more room to expand and better access to nutrients and light.

6. After planting, give the plants a good soaking to help the dirt settle around their roots. Maintain a stable moisture level in the soil without letting it become soggy by watering on a regular basis. Mulch the plants with straw or wood chips to keep the soil moist, prevent weeds, and keep the ground at a consistent temperature.

7. Some vining pumpkin types can be trellised to make more efficient use of space and to improve ventilation, both of which can aid in disease prevention. Train the vines to grow upward using soft ties or twine and a robust trellis or fence system.

In order to guarantee that your pumpkin plants thrive and provide quality fruit, it is important to follow the planting and spacing instructions provided below.

CHAPTER FIVE
How To Maintain Your Pumpkin Plants

The health and yield of pumpkin plants depend on attentive care and upkeep. Throughout the growing season, remember these essential steps:

• Pumpkins need regular watering, especially in the hot and dry summer months. Give the plants an inch or two (2.5 to 5 cm) of water once a week for the best results. Root rot is caused by overwatering, so be careful. To reduce the spread of illness, water the plants only at their bases.

- Mulching: Cover the ground surrounding the plants with a layer of organic mulch, like straw or wood chips. Mulch has multiple purposes: it controls soil temperature, slows down weed development, and helps preserve water. To avoid the spread of illnesses caused by excess moisture, keep the mulch a couple of inches away from the base of the plants.

- Pumpkins are big feeders, therefore they need consistent feedings of fertilizer. Follow the directions on the package to apply a balanced fertilizer, such as a 10-10-10 or 14-14-14 combination. Fertilize the plants once every two to three weeks once they have developed a few genuine leaves.

• Pruning and training entails keeping an eye on the vines as they expand and cutting away any dead or diseased limbs. Diseases are less likely to spread and ventilation is enhanced as a result. You can prune the vines to keep them from encroaching or train them to grow in a specific direction.

• Pollination is necessary for pumpkins to set fruit. It is crucial to encourage bees to your garden because they are the major pollinators of pumpkins. Planting flowers that attract pollinators is a good alternative to using chemicals that could harm bees.

• Check for pests and diseases frequently to keep your pumpkin plants healthy. Powdery mildew, squash bugs, and cucumber beetles are all common pests.

Keep an eye out for pests, and if you spot any, take action like applying organic insecticides or adopting integrated pest management strategies. Spacing plants appropriately, allowing for adequate airflow, and not watering from above can all help reduce the likelihood of illness.

- Maintain a weed-free zone surrounding your pumpkin plants. Pumpkins and weeds are rivals in the struggle for resources. Weeds can be controlled by either regular hand removal or the application of organic mulch.

- To prevent the pumpkins from rotting in the dirt as they grow, prop them up with some clean, soft material, such straw or cardboard. This helps keep the fruit clean and fresh for longer.

- Pumpkins are ready to be picked when they have achieved full size and the skin has hardened. Use a sharp knife to remove the stem, but leave about 3 to 4 inches (7.5 to 10 cm) of the stem connected to the fruit. Avoid damaging the pumpkins by handling them carefully.

By giving your pumpkin plants the attention they need, you can ensure their continued health, boost their yield, and protect them from pests and viruses. Constant observation and prompt action are key to a fruitful crop.

The Gathering And Keeping Of Pumpkins

If you want your pumpkins to taste great and remain fresh for a long time, harvesting and storing practices are essential. How to Pick and Keep Pumpkins for Later Use

1. Pumpkins are harvested at different times depending on the type and the final usage. Pumpkins are ready to be picked after they have achieved their full size, their skin has hardened, and their vines have dried up or died back. For optimal harvest results, follow the advice provided for your chosen variety.

2. Pumpkins can be harvested by cutting them from the vine with a sharp knife or pruning shears and leaving a stem of about 3 to 4 inches (7.5 to 10 cm) in length. Pumpkins can be easily damaged by yanking or twisting them off the vine.

3. Careful Harvesting: Pumpkins should be handled carefully during harvest to avoid bruising or other damage. Rough treatment can cause decay or reduce its shelf life in storage.

4. Pumpkins should be cured for 10-14 days after harvest, in a warm, dry place. The skin's hardness and shelf life are both improved by the curing process. Spread the pumpkins out in a single layer with plenty of space between them.

5. Cleaning: Before putting the pumpkins away, clean them by wiping them down with a damp cloth or sponge to remove any dust or debris. Excess moisture can cause rotting, so only water if absolutely essential.

6. The quality of pumpkins can be maintained for longer if they are stored in the right conditions. The ideal conditions for storing are as follows:

- Pumpkins should be kept in a dry location between 50 and 55 degrees Fahrenheit (10 and 13 degrees Celsius). Keep them away from any sources of heat or regions where the temperature fluctuates, as this can hasten their decomposition.

- Humidity: Keep it between 50 and 70 per cent always. Low humidity can induce shriveling, while high humidity might cause mold or decay. Humidity can be increased in a dry storage location by keeping a tray of water nearby.

- Keep the storage area well-ventilated to reduce the likelihood of mold and mildew growth and the spread of disease. Avoid blocking airflow by placing the pumpkins too closely together.

7. Use crates, wooden boxes, or vented shelves, all of which are ideal for storing pumpkins. To prevent the spread of rot, the pumpkins' containers should provide ventilation and separate them from one another.

8. Inspect the pumpkins on a regular basis to look for symptoms of rot, mold, or decay. It's important to get rid of rotting or diseased pumpkins as soon as possible to stop the spread of the problem.

9. Pumpkins have a rather long shelf life—anywhere from two to three months, depending on the variety and how they're handled. Pumpkins for pies, for example, may not keep as long as other varieties.

It's important to keep in mind that not all pumpkins may be stored for an extended period of time. Pumpkins of the decorative or ornamental variety are better suited for temporary exhibition than long-term storage.

Whether you intend to use your pumpkins for cooking, carving, or decorating, you can get more use out of them by following these harvesting and storing tips.

CHAPTER SIX
Making Use Of Pumpkins

Pumpkins are one of the most useful fruits because of their adaptability. Popular pumpkin applications include:

• Pumpkins have numerous culinary applications and are a popular ingredient. Pumpkins are versatile, and its flesh can be used to make a wide variety of tasty dishes, including soup, pie, bread, muffins, pancakes, and risotto. Another healthy option is to roast pumpkin seeds and eat them.

• Decorating for Halloween and Thanksgiving: Pumpkins, symbols of autumn, are ubiquitous in these holiday traditions. For Halloween, you can carve pumpkins into jack-o'-lanterns or simply utilize them as decorative accents throughout the house. Smaller pumpkins and beautiful varieties are frequently used as centerpieces.

• Pumpkin is a common flavoring for seasonal drinks. Many people look forward to the fall so they may indulge in pumpkin-spiced beverages like lattes, smoothies, and teas.

• Pumpkins are a great source of nutrition for pigs, chickens, and other animals. They are a healthy supplement to animal diets due to their high fiber content and nutritional value. For safety's sake, only use pesticide- and chemical-free pumpkins for this.

• Pumpkin has antioxidants, vitamins, and minerals that are good for the skin, making it a popular ingredient in cosmetics and skin care products. It's great for DIY facial masks, exfoliating body scrubs, and conditioning hair treatments. Pumpkin's enzymes are great for getting rid of dead skin and bringing out your skin's natural radiance.

• When it comes to composting, pumpkins are a great ingredient to include. Their rapid decomposition provides the compost with a nutrient boost. Pumpkins should not be composted if they have been treated with chemicals, wax, or paint.

• Pumpkins grown from heirloom or open-pollinated cultivars can have their seeds saved for subsequent plantings. To save seeds for the next planting season, they should be allowed to grow and dry completely before being cleaned and stored in a cool, dry place.

• Children, in particular, can benefit from the instructional use of pumpkins. Use them in studies including estimation and measurement of weight and circumference, as well as exploration of their anatomy and the germination of seeds.

Always aim for efficiency when working with pumpkins. Make good use of the fruit, compost the leftovers, and find another use for beautiful pumpkins when they have served their original purpose.

Pumpkins are quite versatile thanks to their abundance of uses in the kitchen, at home, and in the garden. Use your imagination, and have fun exploring all the ways you can consume this fantastic fruit.

Fixing The Most Frequent Pumpkin Issues

Although growing pumpkins isn't always easy, many of the most frequent issues can be avoided or dealt with if you pay close enough attention. If your pumpkin is acting up, try these solutions:

• Powdery mildew is a fungus disease characterized by a white, powdery growth on the leaves. Powdery mildew can be avoided by keeping enough space between plants and never watering from above. Powdery mildew should be treated using fungicidal sprays made for that purpose.

- Another fungal disease that can harm pumpkin plants is called downy mildew, and it manifests as fuzzy gray spots on the underside of the leaves and yellow spots on the upper sides. Grow resistant plants by planting them in well-ventilated areas with minimal amounts of overhead watering. In extreme cases of fungal growth, fungicidal sprays may be required.

- A calcium deficit or inconsistent watering can produce blossom end rot, which manifests as a dark, sunken patch at the bottom of the pumpkin. Water regularly to keep soil moisture consistent, add calcium to the soil as needed, and refrain from using too much nitrogen fertilizer.

• Infestations Squash bugs, cucumber beetles, and vine borers are just a few of the common pests that can damage a pumpkin crop. Be on the lookout for wilting, yellowing leaves and egg clusters as telltale symptoms of pest damage to your plants. Use row coverings and other physical barriers to keep pests out, and rely on organic insecticides only when required.

• Inadequate pollination or bad climatic conditions are potential causes of poor fruit set. Planting flowers near your garden will attract pollinators, or you can manually pollinate your plants by brushing pollen from male to female blooms. Fruit production can be boosted by making sure the soil is always adequately hydrated and fed.

• Infection. Don't water too much, and make sure there's adequate drainage. When pumpkins start to turn brown, it's time to pick them. In order to stop the spread of disease, rotten fruit must be removed immediately.

• Disease, pest damage, or environmental stress are only few of the many potential causes of vine dieback. Keep an eye out for any signs of damage or pests, and treat the plants as needed. Make sure the plants get enough water and food to keep them from being stressed.

• Pumpkins can get sunburned if they are left out in the sun for too long, causing the skin to turn a drab shade of yellow or brown. To prevent the pumpkins from being damaged by the sun, create shade or cover them with straw or fabric.

Keep in mind that avoiding typical pumpkin issues requires a focus on prevention. The effects of these problems can be mitigated and the likelihood of a healthy pumpkin harvest increased by providing ideal growing conditions, regular monitoring, and timely action.

CHAPTER SEVEN
Modern Methods For Growing Pumpkins

Modern methods of growing pumpkins allow for more harvests, better plant health, and higher quality produce. Here are some cutting-edge methods that savvy farmers might want to try:

• Growing pumpkins in a high tunnel or greenhouse has many benefits because of the regulated environment. It shields plants from the elements, lengthens the growing season, and reduces the risk of pests and illnesses. It also facilitates more precise control over environmental factors like temperature and humidity, which in turn boosts growth and productivity.

• The use of trellises and other vertical growing structures can prevent pumpkin vines from smothering the ground. Using this method, the vines are trained to ascend along posts, fences, or trellises. Space is conserved, airflow is improved, disease pressure is decreased, and plant management is simplified.

• Pruning and training are methods used to encourage healthy growth and maximize yield from plants. To improve air circulation and light penetration, remove unwanted foliage, lateral branches, and runners on a regular basis. This method decreases the spread of illness and frees up resources for increased fruit output. Vine training has other benefits, including better plant health and more efficient use of available space.

• Pumpkins can be grown intensively by planting them in much smaller rows than is customary. This strategy is called "successive planting." This method optimizes crop production by making the most of available land. Planting multiple pumpkin harvests at intervals throughout the growing season is known as "successive planting." It facilitates continuous harvesting and aids in disease and insect control.

• Implementing a drip irrigation system equipped with timers and moisture sensors enables careful management of watering needs. Using this method, you may keep your soil at its ideal moisture level, save money by using less water, and protect your plants from diseases caused by soggy conditions. Precision nutrient delivery to plants is also possible through the use of fertigation (the administration of fertilizers through irrigation).

• The key to successful pumpkin cultivation is advanced nutrient management, which entails routine soil testing and the implementation of a focused nutrient management program. The results of a soil test can be used to create a fertilizer blend tailored to the plant's unique nutritional requirements. It is also possible to treat nutritional deficits and improve plant health by foliar feeding, which involves applying nutrients directly to the leaves of the plant.

• Effective pest management can be achieved through the use of a variety of techniques, including cultural practices, biological controls, and targeted pesticide applications, all of which go under the umbrella term "integrated pest management" (IPM). Pest populations can be reduced with minimal damage to the environment through the use of trap crops, beneficial insects, and selective pesticide use as well as regular scouting.

• Hand-pollination and the deployment of specialized pollinator colonies are only two examples of the kinds of sophisticated pollination methods that can be used to guarantee successful fruit set.

To pollinate a flower by hand, a little brush or cotton swab is used to move pollen from a male flower to a female blossom. Increasing pollination success by placing honeybee hives or native bee colonies near the pumpkin patch.

- Modern Methods for Managing Diseases Modern methods for managing diseases include planting resistant cultivars, rotating crops, maintaining clean facilities, and strategically applying fungicides. The timely response and effective control of a disease requires constant scouting for the first signs of the sickness.

Keep in mind that these cutting-edge methods can call for more time, money, and knowledge than you now have available. Researching and consulting with seasoned farmers or agricultural experts is a must before using any cutting-edge farming techniques to guarantee success under your unique conditions.

Conclusion

Whether you're a first-time grower or a seasoned pro, pumpkin gardening may be a satisfying and pleasurable experience. Successful pumpkin farming requires knowing the pumpkin life cycle, picking the proper location, preparing the soil, and picking the right types.

Plant health and yields can be improved with the help of regular watering, fertilizing, pest and disease management, and weed control.

Growing pumpkins can be improved with the use of modern techniques such as high-tunnel farming, trellising, intense planting, and sophisticated fertilizer management.

If pumpkins are harvested at the right time and kept in the right conditions, they will retain their quality and last for a longer period of time. Putting pumpkins to use in a variety of ways (culinary, decorative, and otherwise) is the best way to learn to appreciate their many virtues.

Keep in mind that you'll need information, observation, and adaptability to your individual growing conditions in order to solve typical pumpkin difficulties and execute advanced development approaches. Growing pumpkins successfully requires constant study, experimentation, and advice from seasoned farmers and agricultural professionals.

Get your hands dirty and revel in the experience of cultivating and making use of pumpkins, one of autumn's most cherished and recognizable symbols. The best of luck with your pumpkin patch!

THE END

Made in United States
Troutdale, OR
03/15/2025